I0813960

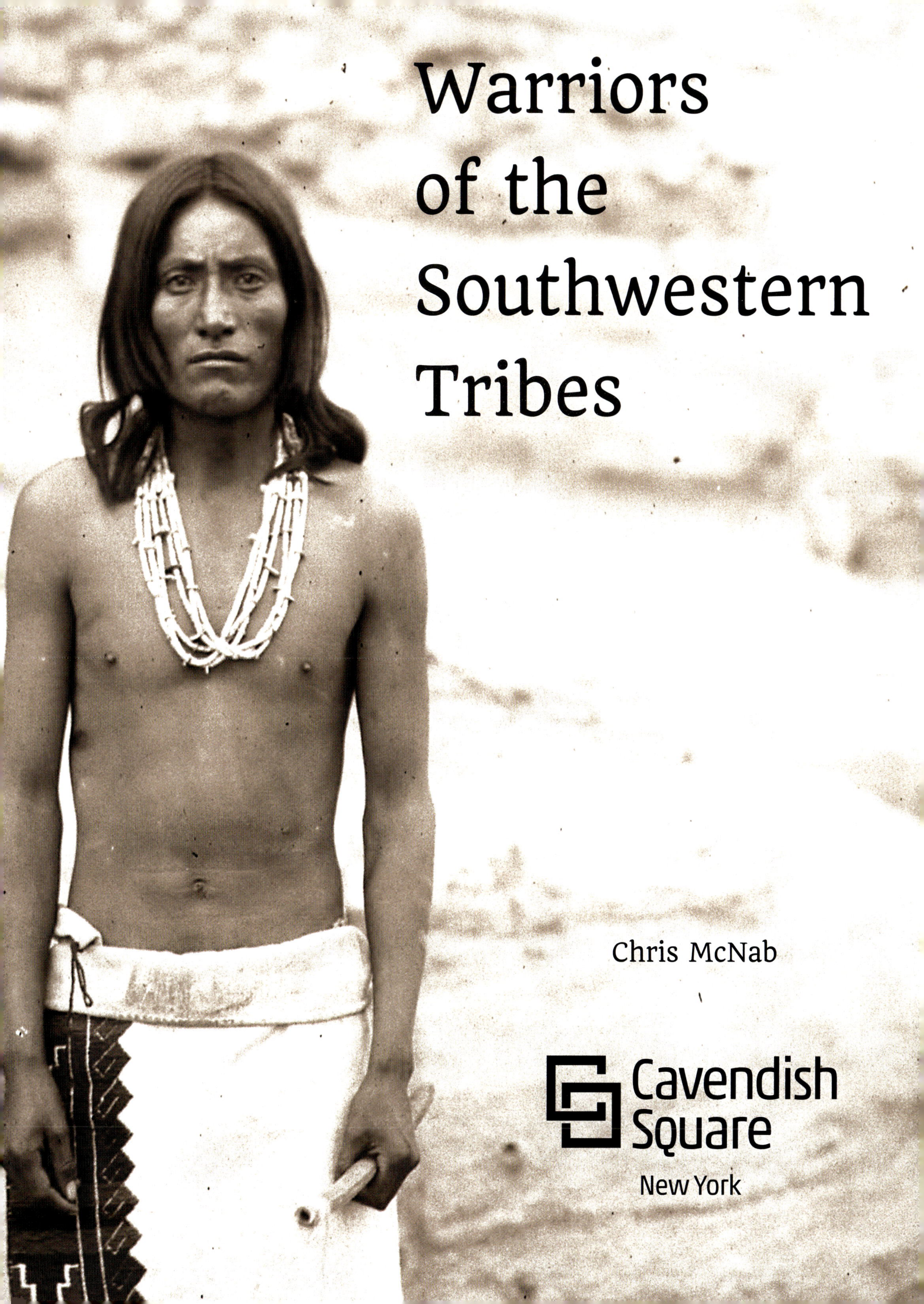

Warriors of the Southwestern Tribes

Chris McNab

Cavendish Square
New York

This edition published in 2018 by Cavendish Square Publishing, LLC
243 5th Avenue, Suite 136, New York, NY 10016

First Edition

Website: cavendishsq.com

Cataloging-in-Publication Data

Names: McNab, Chris, author.
Title: Warriors of the southwestern tribes / Chris McNab.
Description: New York : Cavendish Square Publishing, 2018. | Series: Native American warfare | Includes glossary and index. | Audience: Grades 6–10.
Identifiers: ISBN 9781502632876 (library bound) | ISBN 9781502633156 (ebook)
Subjects: LCSH: Indians of North America—Southwest, New—Juvenile literature.
Classification: LCC E78.S7 M37 2018 | DDC 979.004'97—dc23

Editorial Director: David McNamara
Editor: Megan Kellerman
Associate Art Director: Amy Greenan
Production Coordinator: Karol Szymczuk

The photographs in this book are used by permission and through the courtesy of: All maps and black-and-white line artworks produced by JB Illustrations © Amber Books; AKG Images: 47 & 75 (North Wind Picture Archives), 162 (North Wind Picture Archives); Alamy: 98tr (North Wind Picture Archives); Art Archive: 128/129 (William E. Weiss/Buffalo Bill Historical Center), 194 (Buffalo Bill Historical Center); Bridgeman Art Library: 88/89 (Peter Newark American Pictures), 104/105bl (Peter Newark American Pictures), 120 (Look & Learn), 133 (Peter Newark American Pictures), 135 & 151 (Look & Learn), 174 & 197 (Peter Newark American Pictures); Corbis: 19 & 20 (Bettmann), 22t (Werner Forman Archive), 32 (Robert Wagenhoffer), 39 (Marilyn Angel Wynn/Nativestock Pictures), 42, 55 (Medford Historical Society Collection), 56/57 (Historical Picture Archive), 58 (Historical Picture Archive), 62 (Nik Wheeler), 63, 64, 83 (Bettmann), 86 (Peter Harholdt), 112, 137, 143, 146, 152, 157, 158, 159, 160 (Bettmann), 161 (Poodles Rock), 165tr, 165b (Tria Giovan), 176, 184 (Bettmann), 192 (Werner Forman Archive), 206, 209, 210, 211, 214/215 (Bettmann) Dorling Kindersley: 105t (Geoff Brightling) Getty Images: 8 (Bridgeman Art Library), 11 (Roger Viollet), 15 (Joe Sohm/Visions of America), 25 (Time & Life Pictures), 29 (Marilyn Angel Wynn/Nativestock Pictures), 36, 48 & 74 (Bridgeman Art Library), 78br (Science & Society Picture Library), 79tr & 97 (Hulton Archive), 140 & 145 (Time & Life Pictures), 148 (SuperStock), 150 (Bridgeman Art Library), 170/171 (Hulton Archive), 177 (Hulton Archive), 178 (Marilyn Angel Wynn/Nativestock Pictures), 193 (Bridgeman Art Library), 204/205, 207 (Hulton Archive); iStockphoto: 153 (Duncan Walker); Library of Congress: 9, 12/13, 17, 27tr, 41, 45, 49, 50/51, 54, 59, 65tl, 65b, 70, 72tr, 76, 85tl, 85br, 98bl, 100, 106, 109tl, 111, 115, 117, 118, 119, 121, 125, 127tr, 130, 139, 141 (both), 144, 154/155, 156, 163, 164, 167, 168 & 169 (all), 180 (both), 183 & 183 (both), 185, 187, 188, 195, 198/199, 200, 208; Mary Evans Picture Library: 81, 147, 181; Photos.com: 78/79tl, 90, 91, 109b, 127b, 172, 175; Photoshot: 6/7 (World Illustrated), 22bl & 113 (UPPA), 179 (UPPA); Public Domain: 72bl, 122; TopFoto: 102/103 (Granger Collection), 138 & 191 (Granger Collection); U.S. Department of Defense: 213; Werner Forman Archive: 27b (Ohio State Museum), 202 (Anthropological Museum of Lomonosov, Moscow).

Printed in the United States of America

CONTENTS

Introduction

The Apache and Navajo are justifiably some of the most enduring Native American tribal names in popular memory. Their resistance, and that of several other Southwestern tribes, to the encroachments of the settlers endured well into the late nineteenth century, and can be attributed to a martial spirit and formidable warrior skills.

Most histories of Native American tribes have a sad inevitability about them. The typical pattern that would emerge involved Indian resistance to the encroaching settlers gradually giving way to subjugation or even destruction. Yet the case of the tribes of the American southwest, the Apaches being the most famous, is particularly pitiable. Here we see the Native Americans trapped between the forces of Spain and Mexico to the south and the United States from the east, the friction between Indians and settlers spiraling into grotesque wars in which extermination of the native peoples was often a cornerstone of settler policy. In balance, however, the Indians of the southwest were particularly tenacious foes, with warriors' skills taking a heavy toll on their enemies right until the very end of the nineteenth century.

The geographical focus of this book is essentially on what is today Arizona, Colorado, Mexico, New Mexico, and western Texas. This area incorporated many Native American tribes less well-known to history, including the Zuni, Keres, Piri, and Tiwa, but is principally remembered for one of the most legendary of all Indian peoples—the Apaches (to which the equally famous Navajo were related). While, therefore, this volume will focus heavily on Apache history and warfare, it will also use this great tribe to illuminate the practices of others, such as the Hopi and the Mohave.

◀ **Apache warriors retreat at full gallop following a horse-raiding mission. Back at their camp, the fresh horses acquired during the raid would be distributed equitably among the tribal members.**

CHAPTER 1

Apache Resistance

The Apaches were not a single tribe, but rather, like the Algonquian of the northeastern United States, a body of linguistically related peoples scattered over a fairly wide range of territory. The principal Apache groupings were the Western, Navajo, Chiricahua, Jicarilla, Kiowa, Lipan, and Mescalero, these inhabiting (by the early 1800s) pockets of territory that reached from central Arizona across to the Pecos River in Texas and north to the headwaters of the San Juan River in Colorado. Geographically, the Apache territories varied considerably, from mountains and plains through to arid, inhospitable deserts. The more northerly Apache tribes managed to avoid settler intrusions for some time into the sixteenth century, but for the tribes in the south, blood was soon spilled as they came into contact with the belligerent Spanish.

The Spanish Wars

By the 1540s, Spanish *conquistadors* were making incursions across the Mexican border and up the Rio Grande river, clashing with the Chiricahua and Mescalero Apaches as they went. The colony of New Mexico was established by the 1590s, and its first governor, Juan de Onate, largely set the pattern for future Spanish–Indian relations. Following the killing of a Spanish detachment by Pueblo warriors, de Onate launched a major military expedition

▲ **A poignant photograph of a Pueblo Indian, illustrating the simplicity of dress for which they were known. The Pueblo had to adjust to Spanish, Mexican, and American rule.**

TRIBES OF THE SOUTHWEST CULTURE AREA

Akimel O'odham (*Pima*)
Apache
Cocopa
Cora
Guarijio
Havasupai
Hopi
Hualapai
Huichol
Karankawa
Maricopa
Mayo
Mojave
Navajo
Opata
Pima Bajo
Pueblo
Quechan
Seri
Tarahumara
Tepehuan
Tohono O'odham (*Papago*)
Tubar
Yaqui
Yavapai
Zuni

against the town of Acoma, and on January 24, 1599, his troops massacred some 800 Pueblo citizens and drove another 600 into slavery. For good measure, all male prisoners had one foot amputated.

Yet the Spaniards faced more substantial resistance when they encountered the Apaches. The Apaches resented not only the threat to their territories, but also the destruction of Pueblo communities with whom they traded. Note that the Apaches did not face the Spanish as a homogenous and united body. In fact, even the individual Apache groupings were themselves separated into various families, bands, and clans, coming together in temporary cooperation from time to time when facing a mutual threat. By the seventeenth century, this mutual threat was clearly identified as the Spanish, and from c.1630 the Apaches began a formidable campaign of raiding against Spanish settlements. Contemporary Spanish sources relate how the populations of some settlements were under virtual curfew, unable to venture out after early evening because of the threat of swift death at the hands of lurking Apache bands. Conrad Malte-Brun, an early nineteenth-century ethnographer, wrote a book entitled *Universal Geography* (published in 1829), which in its entry on the Apache peoples provides some additional context to the Indian war with the Spaniards:

"These implacable enemies of the Spaniards infest the whole eastern boundary of this country, from the black mountains to the confines of Cohahuila, keeping the inhabitants of several provinces in an incessant state of alarm. There has never been any thing but short skirmishes with them, and although their number has been considerably diminished by wars and frequent famine, the Spaniards are obliged constantly to keep up an establishment of 2,000 dragoons, for the purpose of escorting their caravans, protecting their villages, and repelling these attacks, which are perpetually renewed. At first the Spaniards endeavored to reduce to slavery those who, by the fate of war, fell into their hands; but seeing them indefatigably surmount every obstacle that opposed their return to their dear native mountains, their conquerors adopted the expedient of sending their

Apache Warrior
The Mescalero Apache warrior here is armed with an exceptionally long lance, decorated with fur sections and feathers, and has a medicine shield for protection. In terms of clothing, he wears a fur turban plus a painted buckskin shirt and buckskin leggings. Southwestern shields were typically made from thick layers of buckskin, and some varieties were even designed to fold down when not in use.

prisoners to the island of Cuba, where, from the change of climate, they speedily perished. No sooner were the Apaches informed of this circumstance than they refused any longer either to give or receive quarter. From that moment none have ever been taken prisoners, except those who are surprised asleep, or disabled during the combat."

– *Malte-Brun* (1829)

Malte-Brun presents a fairly accurate portrayal of the early Spanish–Indian conflict, with the Spaniards having to commit major resources in the New Mexican territories just to ensure the operation of daily life. Furthermore, the passage ends with a reflection on the brutal nature of the conflict, which eventually led Spaniards, Mexicans, and Americans alike to place bounties on Apache scalps collected, including those of women and children.

The Spanish policy of Apache extermination did not play out as intended. Aided by the Pueblo Revolt of 1680, the Apaches managed to eject the Spanish from New Mexico, although the settlers clawed back their territories over the next 12 years and improved security by establishing *presidios* (fortified bases) along their frontier territories. The Apache raids nevertheless continued unabated throughout most of the eighteenth century, until more subtle Spanish

PUEBLO SETTLEMENTS 1700

The Pueblo Indians were, by the beginning of the eighteenth century, spread throughout modern New Mexico and Arizona. Each Pueblo settlement was a distinct social entity, with its own internal system of governance. Yet all the settlements retained cultural and sometimes military alliances.

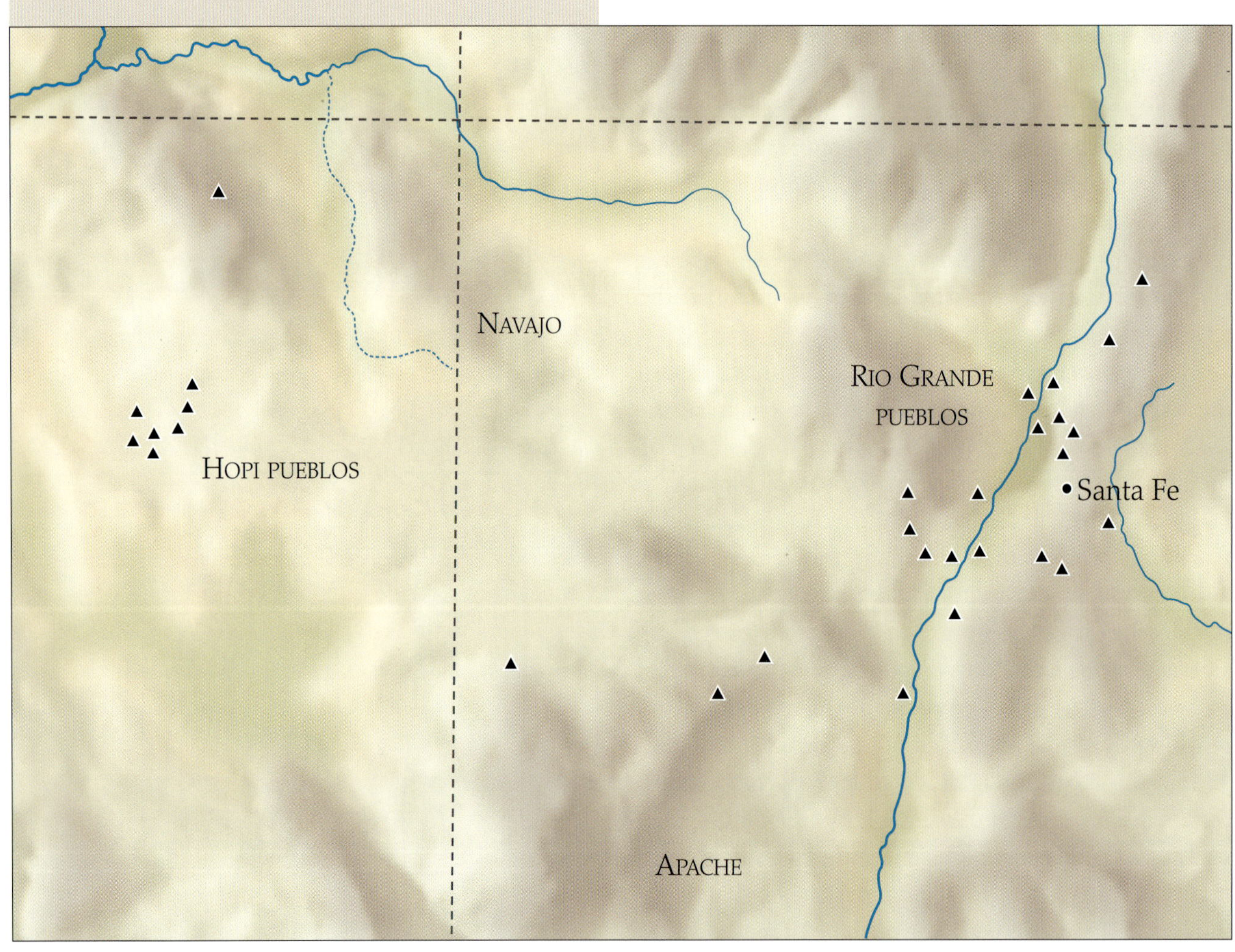

tactics in the 1780s brought greater results. By fostering conflict *between* the Apache tribes, through giving some less belligerent groups preferential Spanish protection, and plying these peoples with alcohol, the Spanish regained a measure of control during the late eighteenth and early nineteenth centuries. Thousands of Apaches entered new, grim lives on the reservations.

▲ **The Pueblo Revolt, 1680. Spanish soldiers turn their swords and firearms on the Pueblo Indians. It took the Spanish 12 years to bring the rebellion fully under control.**

The Effects of Alcohol

The introduction of alcohol by the settlers into Native American society across North America had a significant effect on the ability of the Indians to resist their enemies. Many Native American peoples have a near-allergic reaction to grain alcohol, and the ability to induce stupefaction was quickly appreciated by the settlers during the seventeenth century, when they were more than happy to turn Indians into alcoholics.

APACHE TERRITORY 1800

This map of Apache territory at the beginning of the nineteenth century clearly shows how the Apaches separated out into distinct tribal pockets. Apache groups were found in Arizona, New Mexico, Texas, Mexico, Colorado, and Oklahoma.

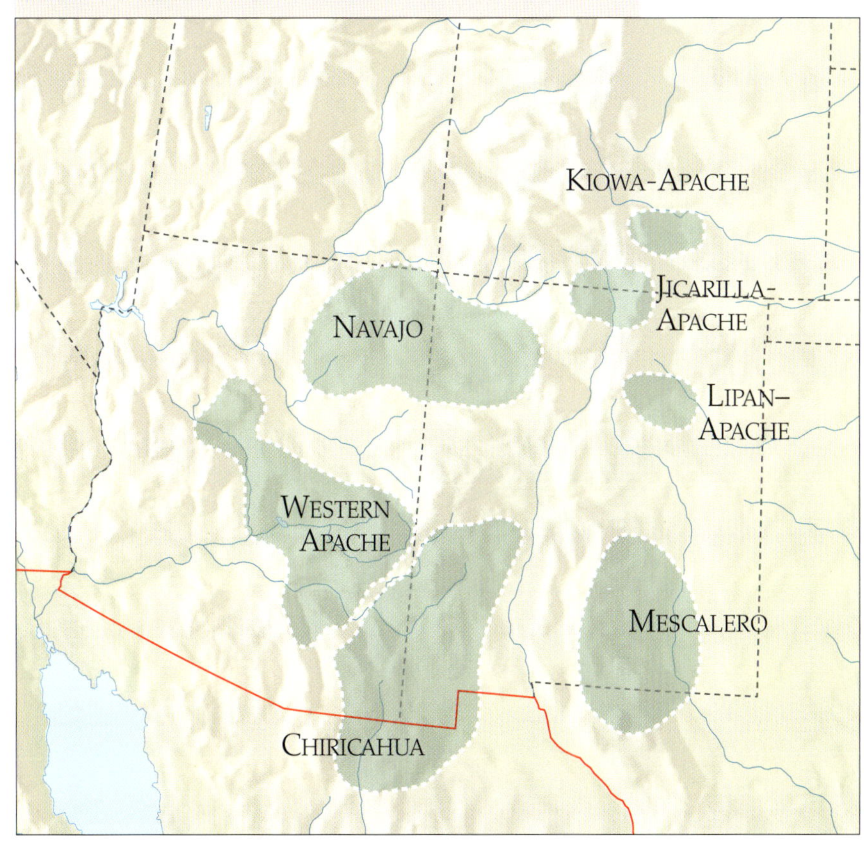

The effects of alcohol are clearly described by the Apache warrior Geronimo, whom we shall encounter later in this chapter. During the 1860s, in one of his operations against the Mexicans, he encountered a mule train with a very special cargo. Here he describes (he provided an autobiography in the early twentieth century) what happened next:

"We attacked several settlements in the neighborhood and secured plenty of provisions and supplies. After about three days we attacked and captured a mule pack train at a place called by the Indians 'Pontoco.' It is situated in the mountains due west, about one day's journey from Arispe.

There were three drivers with this train. One was killed and two escaped. The train was loaded with mescal, which was contained in bottles held in wicker baskets. As soon as we made camp the Indians began to get drunk and fight each other. I, too, drank enough mescal to feel the effect of it, but I was not drunk. I ordered the fighting stopped, but the order was disobeyed. Soon almost a general fight was in progress. I tried to place a guard out around the camp, but all were drunk and refused to serve. I expected an attack from Mexican troops at any moment, and really it was a serious matter to me, for being in command I would be held responsible for any ill luck attending the expedition. Finally the camp became comparatively still, for the Indians were too drunk to walk or even fight. While they were in this stupor I poured out all the mescal, then I put out all the fires and moved the pack mules to a considerable distance from the camp."

– *Barrett* (1906)

The disorder brought about by alcohol, as witnessed in this incident, reached epidemic proportions amongst many Native American tribes, and bred dependence upon European suppliers to feed the subsequent addictions. Alcoholism remains a significant problem amongst Native American peoples even today, with much higher percentage rates of alcohol abuse than many other sectors of American society, a sad legacy of the clash of cultures.

"THE DEEPLY-INGRAINED APACHE HATRED OF THE MEXICANS WAS INTENSIFIED WHEN, IN 1825, THE GOVERNOR OF SONORA OFFERED A BOUNTY OF 100 PESOS ($100) FOR THE SCALP OF ANY APACHE WARRIOR OVER FOURTEEN. THIS BOUNTY WAS IMITATED BY CHIHUAHUA PROVINCE IN 1837, AND WAS EVEN EXTENDED TO 50 PESOS FOR WOMEN'S SCALPS AND 25 PESOS FOR THOSE OF CHILDREN."

– HOOK (1987)

New Enemies

In 1821, Mexico declared its independence from Spain. It was the catalyst for a new wave of hostility between the Apaches and the settlers. Problems arose as the cash-strapped Mexican government let the *presidio* system slide; it also had less cash available to maintain basic living conditions on the Indian reservations. During the 1820s, therefore, Apache raiding became more vigorous, with a particularly insidious response from the Mexicans, as the historian Jason Hook explains in the quotation, left.

A cruel state of warfare existed between the Indians and the Mexicans for the next decade, at which point came a major political change for the region and for the Apaches. The Treaty of Guadalupe Hidalgo, signed in 1848, transferred the southwestern territories to the United States, and established permanent borders between the United States and Mexico. While the treaty was principally focused on territorial divisions and rights of citizenship, its Article XI acknowledged the issue of Indian raiding into Mexican territory:

"Considering that a great part of the territories, which, by the present treaty, are to be comprehended for the future within the limits of the United States, is now occupied by savage tribes, who will hereafter be under the exclusive control of the Government of the United States, and whose incursions within the territory of Mexico would be prejudicial in the extreme, it is solemnly agreed that all such incursions shall be forcibly restrained by the Government of the United States whensoever this may be necessary; and that when they cannot be prevented, they shall be

MANGAS COLORADOS AND THE COPPERMINE MIMBREÑOS

The Coppermine Mimbreños was the name applied to those Apaches who worked in the Mexican copper mines at Santa Rita. Headed by their leader, Juan José Compá, the Indians had apparently stable relations with the local Mexicans. All this changed in 1837, when they, along with Compá, were invited to a feast organized by the American trader James Johnson. Unknown to the Indians as they ate and drank, their feast table was the target of a Mexican howitzer, hidden and loaded with grapeshot. Johnson gave the order for the gun to fire, and the artillery piece and small-arms fire slaughtered the dinner party to a man. The scalps of those killed were then traded for a bounty. Indian retaliation came in the form of Mangas Colorados, an eastern Apache leader known for his physical stature and aggressive warrior spirit. Related to Compá, Colorados vented his fury on the local Mexicans and Americans, killing 22 American miners in one incident alone.

After he was caught and beaten by a similar group of miners in April 1851, Colorados became increasingly violent, ordering the killing of anyone seen wearing a hat (Apaches customarily did not wear hats, so their targets were easily identified).

▲ A fairly accurate representation of Apache warriors on the move. The lead figure appears in much the same attire as Mangas Colorados, including the red bandana and settler-style jacket.

punished by the said Government, and satisfaction for the same shall be exacted in the same way, and with equal diligence and energy, as if the same incursions were meditated or committed within its own territory, against its own citizens."

The treaty was strong in spirit, but initially weak in body. Apache warriors continued to raid across the Mexican border, and US attempts to control this activity were limited. Yet the Apaches were soon having problems with American settlers, particularly from the miners who sought to exploit traditional Apache lands. The Mimbreños warrior chief, Mangas Colorados, (see feature box, above) launched a virtual war on the American settlers, a war in which he found a new ally in the tribal leader of the Central Chiricahua, Cochise. They began what became known as the Apache Wars, which ran in an uneven fashion from 1861 to 1886 and cost hundreds of settler and Native American lives.

The Battle of Apache Pass

For the first four years of the Apache Wars, the Native Americans were aided by a major US distraction in the form of the American Civil War. The first Apache–American battle, however, came in 1862, when General James Henry Carleton and his California Volunteers campaigned against the Confederates in New Mexico and Arizona. On July 14, a column of 140 Union troops of the 1st California Cavalry entered the Apache Pass in southern Arizona, confident that they could move through to pass unhindered by the local Apache warriors—negotiations three weeks earlier saw the Apaches give assurances that they could pass through their territory. Once the troops had entered Apache Pass, however, a large Apache force, headed by Colorados and Cochise and aided by future warrior luminaries such as Victorio and Geronimo, attacked, sniping at them from elevated positions. Despite being dehydrated and exhausted, the American troops fought back with dash, elevating

▶ Cochise (1823–74) was one of the greatest of the Apache warrior chiefs. During the 1860s and 1870s, he led his warriors against the Arizona settlers, often disappearing into Mexico to escape pursuers.

AMERICAN EXPANSION 1818–53

The first half of the nineteenth century saw major changes in both the patterns of settler expansion and the political ownership of the country. By the 1850s, the southwest was essentially under US control, the Americans having acquired territory from the Mexicans through war and treaty.

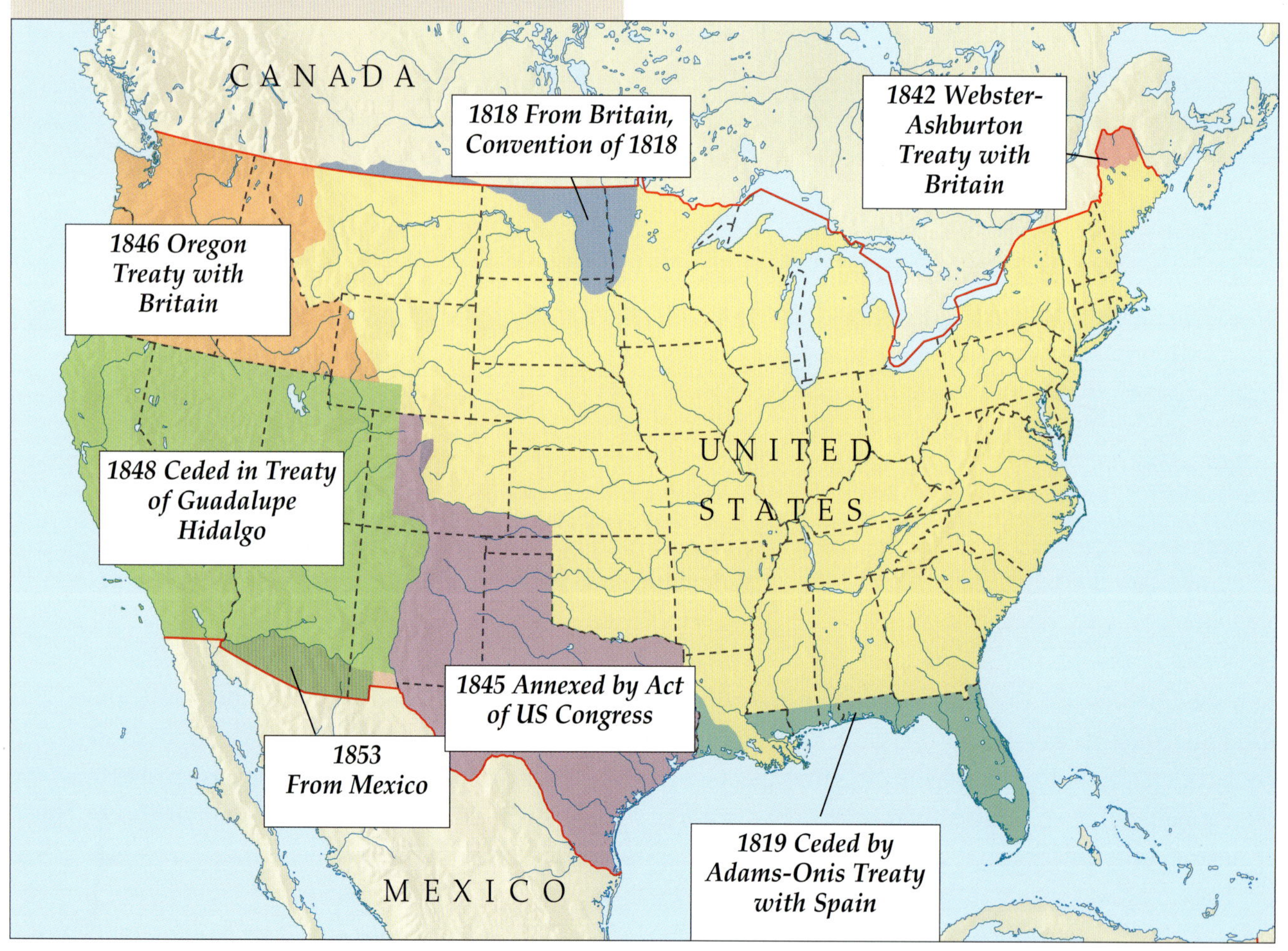

▲ **The Apache Indian chief Victorio (1825–80), here photographed in 1877, was an experienced warrior by the time he reached 20 years old and, after a life of war, died in battle in 1880.**

Apache brands into an anti-US coalition, while the US invested in strengthening its defenses in the region, including the building of Fort Bowie to guard Apache Pass.

Following the Battle of Apache Pass, Carleton's campaigns against the Indians sharpened, and the levels of brutality increased. Colorados was captured and tortured to death in 1863, and Carleton employed the ruthlessly effective Colonel Christopher "Kit" Carson in a war to subdue the Navajo and Mescalero, forcing thousands of them into the Bosque Rendondo Reservation (essentially a brutal prison camp). Carson waged a localized version of total war on the Native Americans, attacking their sources of food and tribal supply lines. His campaign resulted in the "Long Walk" of the Navajo, a forced exodus of 300 miles (482 kilometers) undertaken by 9,000 people, mostly traveling on foot. Hundreds died of exhaustion or execution on the journey, and many more died in the appalling conditions at the Bosque Redondo. The Long Walk was one of the most shameful episodes of the Apache Wars, and cast a lasting shadow over Carson's reputation.

their howitzers and blasting the positions above them. The fight petered out inconclusively, with about 10 Apache dead compared to two Union fatalities, but it had the effect of drawing the various

Crook's Campaigns

The US Government and Army constructed a number of camps and reservations throughout the southwest, designed to contain and assimilate compliant Native Americans. Being in a reservation, however, did not

THE MOHAVE INDIANS

Away from the Apache territories, inhabiting the Arizona–California border, the Mohave Indians also underwent a traumatic social transformation during the mid- to late nineteenth century. During the 1850s, the Mohave were at war both with rival Native American tribes—particularly the Maricopa, Pima, and Papago—and the US settlers who moved into Mohave territory in search of gold, the former conflict weakening the Mohave's capabilities to fight the latter. Mohave attacks on settlers resulted in the US Government establishing protective forts and deploying significant numbers of troops. A major clash between the Mohave warriors and soldiers of the US 6th Infantry brought a signal defeat for the Indians, and their power gradually attenuated during the rest of the century as they were progressively forced onto reservations.

▲ A group of Mohave Indians pose for the camera, armed with a mixture of carbines, rifles, and handguns. The Mohave clashed in some bitter battles with settler gold prospectors.

▲ **Resettled Navajos use adobe bricks to construct living quarters for Union soldiers while under armed guard. The location is the remote Bosque Redondo, a place notorious for its inhumane conditions for Indian captives.**

necessarily ensure protection from settler violence. On the morning of April 30, 1871, a large gang of local American vigilantes descended on the Apache inhabitants of Camp Grant, an ill-guarded US military base. Although the camp was, at the time of the attack, inhabited mainly by old people, women, and children, this did not stop the vigilantes clubbing or shooting to death 117 people, based on their belief that the Camp Grant Indians were responsible for attacks on settlers around southern Arizona.

The US Government responded by establishing its "peace policy," which basically involved forced resettlement of Apache tribes on more reservations. The Navajos and various other Indian tribes signed peace treaties with the Federal Government, although the terms of mutual respect accorded by the legalistic language of the treaties fell far short in reality. Led by General George Crook, the commander of the Department of Arizona, US forces in the region conducted pitiless campaigns against those Apaches who proved stubbornly resistant. Crook had a talent for turning the Apaches against one another, employing large numbers of allied Apache scouts to help track down the enemy war parties hiding in the wilderness. The use of such scouts effectively removed the invisibility that was so important to the Apache style of warfare.

US Army Indian Scouts

It is worthwhile at this point making a deeper study of the US Army Indian Scouts. Scouts were not just recruited from the southwest, but the Apaches,

Article I of the Treaty between the United States of America and the Navajo Tribe of Indians, concluded June 1, 1868

From this day forward all war between the parties to this agreement shall for ever cease. The government of the United States desires peace, and its honor is hereby pledged to keep it. The Indians desire peace, and they now pledge their honor to keep it.

If bad men among the whites, or among other people subject to the authority of the United States, shall commit any wrong upon the person or property of the Indians, the United States will, upon proof made to the agent and forwarded to the Commissioner of Indian Affairs at Washington city, proceed at once to cause the offender to be arrested and punished according to the laws of the United States, and also to reimburse the injured persons for the loss sustained.

If bad men among the Indians shall commit a wrong or depredation upon the person or property of any one, white, black, or Indian, subject to the authority of the United States and at peace therewith, the Navajo tribe agree that they will, on proof made to their agent, and on notice by him, deliver up the wrongdoer to the United States, to be tried and punished according to its laws; and in case they wilfully refuse so to do, the person injured shall be reimbursed for his loss from the annuities or other moneys due or to become due them under this treaty, or any others that may be made with the United States. And the President may prescribe such rules and regulations for ascertaining damages under this article as in his judgment may be proper; but no such damage shall be adjusted and paid until examined and passed upon by the Commissioner of Indian Affairs, and no one sustaining loss whilst violating, or because of his violating, the provisions of this treaty or the laws of the United States shall be reimbursed therefore.

▲ **Samuel F. Tappan, a signatory on the 1868 Navajo Treaty. Tappan was actually an activist for Native American rights, arguing that civil, not military, law should prevail on the reservations.**

▲ **Manuelito was one of several Navajo chiefs who put their names to the 1868 treaty. By the time he signed the treaty, he had been fighting the American settlers for more than a decade.**

US Army Apache Scout
This US Army Apache Scout wears sergeant's stripes, the highest rank typically achieved by Native Americans in US Army employ. He would, however, have little authority over white troops.

Mohave, and Navajo were all fertile recruiting grounds. Other Native American tribes that provided significant numbers of scouts included the Pawnee, Crow, Osage, Arikara, Seminole, and Delaware. The authorization to recruit Indian scouts came with a Congressional Act of July 28, 1866, which stated that:

"The President is authorized to enlist and employ in the Territories and Indian country a force of Indians not to exceed one thousand to act as scouts, who shall receive the pay and allowances of cavalry soldiers, and be discharged whenever the necessity for further employment is abated, at the discretion of the department commander."

Indian Scouts enlisted for a specified period, typically five years, although on discharge they could re-enlist after a period of three to six months. The US Army Indian Scouts should not be confused with civilian Indian military contractors, who were also called scouts. A civilian scout was a temporary employee of the military forces, and had no rights to obtain rank or to receive a military pension. The military scouts, by contrast, could receive a pension and could also ascend a limited way up the NCO rank ladder.

Indian Scouts' Uniform

The uniform of Indian Scouts varied widely depending on the time and place of their service. Generally speaking, the evolution from 1866 to 1895, when the Indian Scouts were finally merged into the US Army, was from civilian dress embellished with the odd military item through to a formal uniform based on that of the US Army. A scout of 1890, for example, might be seen in a five-button fatigue jacket plus matching trousers, all Army issue, and in that year Apache scouts and others were issued with the US Army Dress Helmet, with an appearance similar to that of a British policeman.

The Indian Scouts, as we have seen, were an integral part of the American military campaign to subdue warring Native Americans. Although their position in Native American history is morally ambiguous, they did lay the groundwork for thousands of Native Americans who went on to serve in the US Armed Forces during the twentieth century.

▲ **This group of Indian Scouts presents a mixed bag of clothing and weapons. Although the man on the left has a breechloading carbine, the others are equipped with old muzzle-loading percussion cap rifles.**

Geronimo

During the 1870s, the policy of resettlement had brought nothing but hardship and acrimony for the Native Americans, which in turn sowed the seeds for further revolt and conflict. Apache leaders such as Victorio, Juh, and Geronimo fled from the massive San Carlos reservation, taking with them large groups of followers and waging an insurgency campaign against Crook's men. Geronimo in particular headed the last great resistance of the Apache Wars. More correctly known by the Indian name of Goyathlay ("One Who Yawns"), Geronimo cut his teeth as a warrior acting as a guide for raids against the Mexicans. He first fled the San Carlos reservation in September 1881, then returned in April 1882 as a raider, killing the chief of police there and fleeing back into the wilderness, taking more warriors with him. Over the next four years, Geronimo was repeatedly captured by, or surrendered

▲ A striking portrait of the great Geronimo. Geronimo fought US and Mexican settlers for several decades, and his talents as a warrior are remembered in the motto of the US Army 501st Infantry Regiment—"Geronimo."

to, US troops, only to escape reservation life and return to resistance. In his autobiography, dictated to S. M. Barrett in the early twentieth century, he acknowledged that the US forces had become particularly good at countering his evasive style of warfare:

"Contrary to our expectations the United States soldiers had not left the mountains in Mexico, and were soon trailing us and skirmishing with us almost every day. Four or five times they surprised our camp. One time they surprised us about nine o'clock in the morning, and captured all our horses (nineteen in number) and secured our store of dried meats. We also lost three Indians in this encounter. About the middle of the afternoon of the same day we attacked them from the rear as they were passing through a prairie—killed one soldier, but lost none ourselves. In this skirmish we recovered all our horses except three that belonged to me. The three horses that we did not recover were the best riding horses we had."

– *Barrett* (1906)

Geronimo's flight finally came to an end in September 1886, when he surrendered for the last time. His surrender brought to a close half a century of war between the Apaches and the Americans. The Apaches had been finally quieted, but only at the cost of much American, Mexican, and Spanish blood.

▼ Under military supervision at the desolate San Carlos Reservation, Apaches dig an irrigation ditch as part of a plan to turn what was a nomadic tribe into sedentary farmers. Such forced lifestyles generated much resistance from the Apache people.

CHAPTER 2

Apache Tactics

▲ **White Mountain Apache are mustered at a Southern Pacific Railway Station by a US Army officer for the pursuit of the hostile Apache chief Geronimo. Such scouts were essential for catching the wily outlaw.**

By now we have become somewhat familiar with the impressive physical powers of the Native Americans. The Indians of the southwest, however, took endurance and affinity with the wilderness to near-supernatural levels. From the earliest age, Southwest Indian children, male and female, were acclimatized to the realities of their natural surroundings. For the boys, this process of hardening not only served the purposes of hunting, but also those of warfare:

"The Apaches were trained for war from boyhood. Boys woke early and bathed in the river, even if they had to crack the surface ice to do so. They ran up hillsides and back with a mouthful of water, to learn correct breathing through the nose, and the endurance so characteristic of the Apaches. Boys were hardened by rough wrestling games and mock battles, and taught by their relatives the geography, attributes, and sanctity of their surroundings."

– *Hook (1987)*

Tactical Withdrawals

Such conditioning created young male warriors with an impressive and wide-ranging understanding of the landscape and exceptional powers of endurance. The latter were an integral part of Southwest Indian warfare, as they gave a whole new meaning to the military term "tactical withdrawal." A common ploy of the Southwest Indians was to engage the enemy in a brief, furious ambush and then melt like ghosts back into the landscape. Spanish, Mexican, or American troops would often then set off in pursuit of their enemy, but were actually falling into a trap.

▲ **An Apache raiding party heads out. Such parties were generally kept small—fewer than a dozen people—as it was easier to gain the advantage of surprise with fewer numbers in tow.**

The Indian warriors, who could comfortably cover tens of miles on foot every day, even under the blistering desert sun, would keep the enemy pursuit alive through providing tantalizing glimpses and signs.

Meanwhile, the less-hardened settlers would begin to suffer from exhaustion and dehydration, leaving them exposed to a sudden counter attack when they were least able to resist it. Once the settlers were in retreat, however, the Indians were just as inexhaustible in their pursuit, harrying their enemy constantly and killing or capturing any individuals who strayed far from the group.

The Southwest Indians soon understood that the settlers were not at home in the wilderness they attempted to colonize, and turned this to their advantage. For example, during feigned retreats, the Indians would deliberately create zigzagging and convoluted routes for the pursuers, taking them away from frequently traveled, familiar trails and into countryside where large amounts of equipment became an encumbrance, commanders became disoriented and wagons became stuck or damaged.

The exhaustion and confusion of hunting the Southwest Indians is nowhere more eloquently described than in John G. Bourke's *On the Border with Crook*, published in 1891. Bourke's accounts of fighting the Apache reveals something of why the Apache Wars dragged on for such a long time:

"No serpent can surpass him in cunning; he will dodge and twist and bend in all directions, boxing the compass, doubling like a fox, scattering his party the moment a piece of rocky ground is reached over which it would, under the best circumstances, be difficult to follow. Instead of moving in file, his party will here break into a skirmishing order, covering a

▲ **Apaches brandish their weapons as they charge into an attack. The rocky terrain of the arid southwest provided perfect opportunities for channeling enemies into narrow passes and defiles.**

broad space and diverging at the most unexpected moment from the primitive direction, and not perhaps reuniting for miles. Pursuit is retarded and very frequently baffled ... In the meantime the Apache raiders, who know full well that the pursuit must slacken for a while, have reunited at some designated hill, or near some spring or 'water tank,' and are pushing across the high mountains as fast as legs harder than leather can carry them ... At the summit of each ridge, concealed behind rocks or trees, a few picked men, generally not more than two or three, will remain waiting for the approach of the pursuit."

– *Bourke* (1891)

From this description, it becomes apparent why the settlers had to turn to Indian Scouts to pursue the Apaches and other Southwest Indians. As General Crook once commented, "To polish a diamond, there is nothing like its own dust." Bourke goes on to explain the purpose of the small rearguard groups of Apache, noting that as the pursuers approached they would open fire with firearms or bows for a few seconds, causing the soldiers to halt, bunch up and go to ground. While the soldiers waited to see how the attack would play out, the Apache were back on their feet or horses, and moving quickly away from the scene. By playing this tactic out repeatedly, the settlers' units were compelled to move in fits and starts, exhausting themselves in the process. Probing attacks delivered at night also ensured that the settlers did not get any rest when the sun fell.

Ambush

As with so many Indian tactics, the tactical withdrawal was often the build-up to a deliberate ambush. Much of the territory of the southwest was

COMMUNICATIONS
In his account of the battle against the Apache, John G. Bourke also relates how the Apache communicated with one another during their operations. They relied heavily on ground signals to coordinate their actions against a common enemy, typical signals being the following:

- An inscription or pictograph drawn on the bark of a sycamore tree.
- An inscription or pictograph drawn on a smooth-faced rock, often beneath an overhanging ledge to protect the image from the elements.
- A knot tied in a flexible branch or clump of grasses.
- One or several stones placed against the trunk of a tree.
- A sapling leaned up against another tree.
- A piece of buckskin laid over a branch.

usefully describes the process of ambushing a column of Mexican troops in the Sierra de Sahuaripa Mountains during the summer of 1860:

"The second day in these mountains our scouts discovered mounted Mexican troops. There was only one company of cavalry in this command, and I thought that by properly surprising them we could defeat them. We ambushed the trail over which they were to come. This was at a place where the whole company must pass through a mountain defile. We reserved fire until all of the troops had passed through; then the signal was given. The Mexican troopers, seemingly without a word of command, dismounted, and placing their horses on the outside of the company, for breastworks, made a good fight against us. I saw that we could not dislodge them without using all our ammunition, so I led a charge."

– *Barrett (1906)*

eminently suitable for ambush tactics, with high, rocky terrain split by narrow passes that formed natural choke points for anybody traveling through the territory. Simultaneous fire was the key to an effective ambush, made more so by the prodigious talents of the Southwest Indians with bows and firearms. The typical ambush involved a group of one or two dozen warriors, positioned strategically along a pass or trail. Much like modern anti-tank tactics, the Indians would wait for the enemy column to enter the "kill zone," at which point they would unleash coordinated fire, targeting officers and those manning heavy weapons in particular.

The Apache Geronimo has, as we have seen, done historians a great service by leaving his autobiography to posterity. In his account, he

The description of the ambush illustrates how ammunition conservation was always a consideration

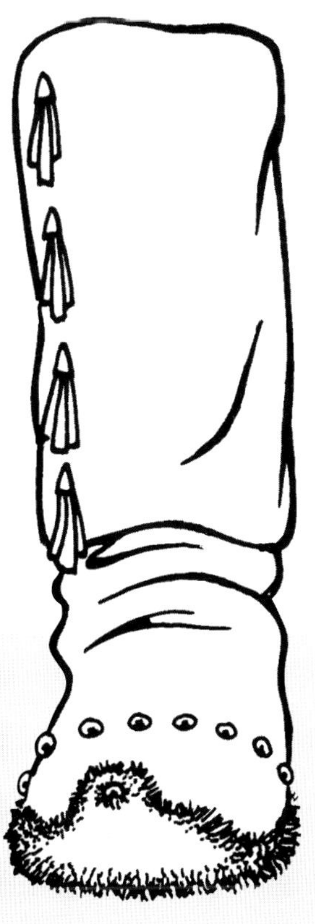

APACHE MOCCASINS
Apache moccasins were not simply warm, durable footwear—their tough rawhide soles provided good adhesion when climbing across rocks, and created near silent footfalls when stalking or escaping from an enemy. The uppers were made from soft buckskin, and decorated with beads and tassels.

▲ ***Apache Ambush*—a painting by Frederic Remington. The Apache, like many Native Americans, proved to be excellent marksmen, a lifetime's training with the bow bringing a natural sense of accuracy.**

for the Indians, and anything more than a small party of enemies would probably require some element of hand-to-hand fighting to destroy. His explanation of the Mexican response also indicates that the settlers were gradually becoming accustomed to the ambush tactic, learning the correct response of finding immediate cover from which to deliver heavy return fire. Geronimo goes on to explain the close-quarters clash that followed:

"The warriors suddenly pressed in from all sides and we fought hand to hand. During this encounter I raised my spear to kill a Mexican soldier just as he leveled his gun at me; I was advancing rapidly, and my foot slipping in a pool of blood, I fell under the Mexican trooper. He struck me over the head with the butt of his gun, knocking me senseless. Just at that instant a warrior who followed in my footsteps killed the Mexican with a spear. In a few minutes not a Mexican soldier was left alive. When the Apache war-cry had died away, and their enemies had been scalped, they began to care for their dead and wounded. I was found lying unconscious where I had fallen. They bathed my head in cold water and restored me to consciousness. Then they bound up my wound and the next morning, although weak from loss of blood and suffering from a severe headache, I was able to march on the return to Arizona. I did not fully recover for months, and I still wear the scar given me by that musketeer. In this fight we had lost so heavily that there really was no glory in our victory, and we returned to Arizona. No one seemed to want to go on the war path again that year."

– *Barrett* (1906)

The vigor, surprise, and violence of the Apache ambush results in the complete destruction of the Mexican force, although Geronimo's experience illustrates that all such attacks carried major risks of their own.

As we have seen above in our analysis of the Apaches, ambush tactics were not always successful—if the settler troops could bring their typically superior firepower to bear, then the battle could be tipped in their favor. Even if the overall outcome of an ambush was positive, heavy return fire from the ambushed soldiers could turn an Indian victory into a pyrrhic one. For example, in late March 1854, soldiers of the US 1st Cavalry Regiment in New Mexico made a patrol out from their camp at Cantonment Burgwin, some 10 miles (16 km) southeast of Taos. During the patrol, a unit of 1st Dragoons, 60 men strong, launched an unauthorized attack on a Jicarilla Apache camp near Pilar, inciting the wrath of local Apache and Ute Indians. In response, the Indians prepared an ambush for the American soldiers, gathering some 200 warriors for the purpose.

The Indians took up position in an area of ravine-split terrain, and at around 8:00 a.m. on March 30, a coordinated war whoop split the morning silence as the Indians unleashed musket and bow fire on the passing American column. Contemporary accounts of the subsequent battle are somewhat contradictory, but we know that the clash lasted between two and four hours and resulted in the US column suffering 22 dead and 36 wounded—a casualty rate approaching 100 percent. Twenty-two horses were also lost. The ambush was in one sense an emphatic victory for the Indian warriors, but the battle cost them around 50 warriors killed, and an unknown number wounded.

▲ Apaches attacking refugees from Santa Rita. Those captured by the Apache faced either immediate execution, imprisonment (typically reserved for women or children), or, less commonly, a slow death by torture back in the Apache village.

The Battle of Skeleton Cave

The firepower possessed by the settlers during the second half of the nineteenth century meant

THE APACHE WAY OF WAR

A useful insight into the Apache way of war came from the pen of Miguel Venegas, whose *A Natural and Civil History of California* of 1759 contains a useful description of not only the Apache treatment of prisoners, but also of their clothing, tactics, and martial character:

"According to some prisoners who have been ransomed, they are extremely savage and brutal; they have very little cultivated land, nor does their country supply them with any plenty of spontaneous productions. They are cruel to those who have the misfortune to fall into their hands; and among them are several apostates. They go entirely naked, but make their incursions on horses of great swiftness, which they have stolen from other parts, a skin serving them for a saddle. Of the same skins they make little boots or shoes of one piece; and by these they are traced in their flight. They begin the attack with shouts, at a great distance, to strike the enemy with terror. They have not naturally any great share of courage; but the little they can boast of, is extravagantly increased on any good success. In war they rather depend on artifice than valour; and on any defeat submit to the most ignominious terms, but keep their treaties no longer than suits their conveniency. His majesty has ordered, that if they require peace, it should be granted; and even offered to them before they are attacked. But this generosity they construe to proceed from fear. Their arms are the common bows and arrows of the country. The intention of their incursions is plunder, especially horses, which they use both for riding and eating; the flesh of these creatures being one of their greatest dainties."

—*Venegas* (1759)

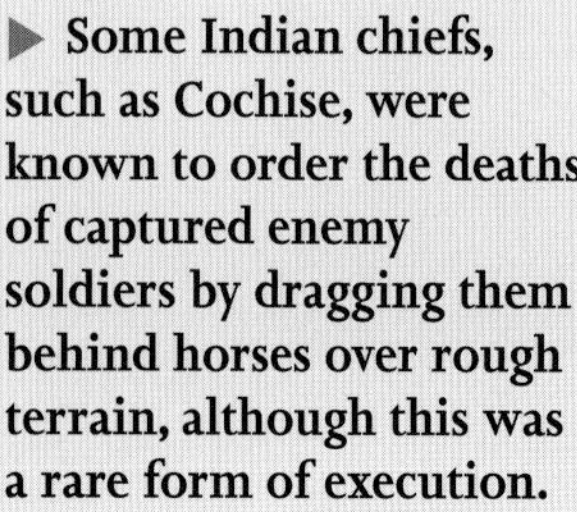

▶ Some Indian chiefs, such as Cochise, were known to order the deaths of captured enemy soldiers by dragging them behind horses over rough terrain, although this was a rare form of execution.

On December 28, 1872, Crook's force—which consisted of three companies of the 5th Cavalry under Captain William H. Brown and utilized the skills of 30 Indian Scouts—finally detected a body of some 110 Yavapai hiding in the mouth of the large Skeleton Cave (also known as Skull Cave) high up in Salt River Canyon.

The American troops surrounded the cave, and when the Indians went to leave Brown announced his presence, and ordered the Indians to surrender. They refused, retreating quickly back into the large cave with American bullets whizzing around their ears. Once inside the recesses of the cave, the Yavapai felt confident of their survival, as the Americans could not see their targets properly to shoot with any real accuracy.

▲ Tombstone, Arizona, 1886. This rare photograph shows the Apache leader Geronimo (*left*), seated in conference with General George Crook on the far right. Geronimo escaped from Crook's custody on two occasions, much to Crook's embarrassment.

that even positions offering apparently excellent cover could be vulnerable. For example, in June 1871 General Crook was appointed to suppress the Indians of Arizona, including those of the Yavapai tribe. The Yavapai were a relatively small group of Indians who had historically allied themselves with the Northern Tonto Apache tribe. Hence when Crook set out on his mission of subjugation, the Yavapai also became targets.

Recognizing this fact, however, Brown ordered his troops to fire their weapons at the roof and walls of the cave, thus producing hails of ricochets that tore into the ranks of the sheltering Indians. The effect was ghastly—a total of 76 Indians died and 37 were wounded. Those who surrendered began life imprisonment or the move to reservations. In this instance, their knowledge of the terrain provided the Indians with no relief from the potent firepower possessed by the Federal Army.

CHAPTER 3

Warfare and Raiding

As historians such as Jason Hook have described, the Apache Indians made a distinction between the practices of "warfare" and "raiding." The purpose of the former was essentially to unleash death upon the enemy, while the latter had the customary objectives of obtaining food, settling scores, and so on, as we have already seen.

Warfare

Open warfare between Southwestern tribes could follow quite formulaic patterns, and frequently involved individual combat among prestigious warriors. In an account of one battle between Yuma and Maricopa Indians in 1842, the Yuma Indians formed themselves into a battle-line headed by two of their chiefs, who walked in front. In contrast to the tactics of evasion and escape described above, here the Yumas approached the Mariocopa village (their objective) quite openly, the two sides forming up in opposing battle lines. When the warriors had gathered, one of the Yuma chiefs stood in front of his Mariocopa counterpart, and offered a challenge. The two men then engaged in single combat, resulting in the death of the Yuma chief, at which point the battle became general, with the respective lines engaging one another. On other occasions, the general clash between opposing sides might actually be resolved by individual or small-group combat, rather than risk the killing of too many warriors in a prolonged battle.

The tribes of the southwest frequently made alliances with one another for purposes of strengthening their warmaking capability. The process of negotiating these alliances was, as one writer of the early nineteenth century described, an activity laced with etiquette and ritual:

"In the organization of war-parties, composed of warriors of the different tribes, certain ceremonies of negotiation are observed. Any band wishing to go to war sends messengers, asking its friends to furnish warriors for an expedition. This mission bears with it the council pipe, and is accompanied by ponies as presents, to encourage the favorable consideration of the proposition. A council is held in which the whole matter is fully discussed. If the band accepts the pipe and smokes, the request is granted, and the warriors of the band, or rather such as choose, extend their co-operation. After this ceremony, warriors from all the bands rendezvous at a given point, and start upon their errand of atrocity and spoliation. To decline acceding to the proposition to take the war-path, frequently occurs from policy or necessity. The band

▼ Apaches on horseback, photographed in the late nineteenth century. The effect of the settlers on the Apache way of life was profound. Previously, the Apache had enjoyed the freedom of vast tracts of land, across which they hunted and journeyed. The settler expansion caused the collapse of Apache culture.

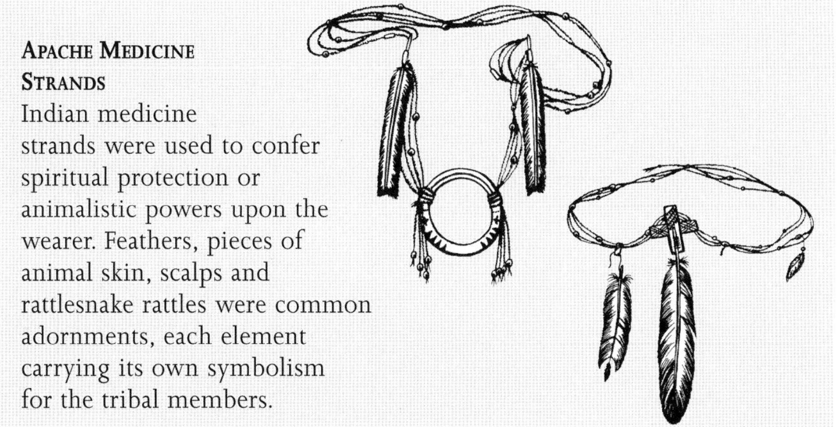

APACHE MEDICINE STRANDS
Indian medicine strands were used to confer spiritual protection or animalistic powers upon the wearer. Feathers, pieces of animal skin, scalps and rattlesnake rattles were common adornments, each element carrying its own symbolism for the tribal members.

seeking for assistance, if not successful in gathering a sufficient number of warriors to make up the necessary strength, abandons its project."

– *Keim* (1825)

The process of making an allied war party is here seen as a delicate matter of mutual respect, but also of reason—the band approached for the alliance considers its position carefully, and it is obvious that there was not an automatic guarantee that a request for an alliance would be granted. War parties of any description were highly ritualistic affairs, preceded by much ceremony. In Apache warmaking, the village shaman would conduct various rites before the party set off, the sage chanting prayers for safety and success. He would also accompany the war party on its outward journey to battle, ensuring that his magic accompanied the fighters all the way to their objective. The warriors also carried small buckskin bags holding a yellow powder known as *hoddentin*, made from the pollen of the cattail, a plant sacred to the Apache. The substance had broad ceremonial applications, ranging from the healing of the sick through to puberty ceremonies for adolescent Apache girls. When setting out on a raid or heading for a battle, each Apache warrior would hold up a small amount of the *hoddentin* to the sun or rub some on his body or tongue.

The shaman watched over any adolescents who were accompanying a war party for the first time. Such boys were blessed by scatterings of *hoddentin* when they left the camp, and the shaman also issued special blessed items of clothing, such as a war cap. The novice warrior was essentially on probation for the first four raids he went on. At first his role was supportive only—he would go and fetch food and water for the other warriors, and act as a guard over the camp at night. If he performed well over the course of the first four raids, he was granted full warrior status, and entered the ranks of the other Apache fighting men.

Raiding

When it came to raiding, the Southwestern Indians conducted their operations in largely the same manner as other Indian tribes. A particularly effective strategy used by the Apaches against the settlers was to raid several locations at once, thereby confusing the required coordinated response. Bourke mentions this strategy, which he saw as particularly acute during the winter of 1870 and the spring of 1871:

"The enemy resorted to a system of tactics which had often been tried in the past and always with success. A number of simultaneous attacks were made at points widely separated, thus confusing both troops and settlers, spreading a vague sense of fear over all the territory infested, and imposing upon the soldiery an exceptional amount of work of the hardest possible kind."

– *Bourke* (1891)

▲ **Navajo shamans gather in full ceremonial outfits to perform a ritual. The settlers attempted to discourage shamanism, which as the Ghost Dance rebellion of the 1890s proved, could be a focus for Indian resistance.**

▶ ***Hoddentin* powder, sprinkled over the face of this Native American woman, was typically used for ritualistic purposes. It was believed to hold a variety of spiritual powers, from bringing protection to a warrior to the healing of the sick.**

Raids in the southwest could range in scale from a dozen warriors stealing a neighboring tribe's horses up to a major action against a well-defended settler outpost. One of the largest raids ever found on record was that attempted by the Navajo Indians in April 1860 against the US Army outpost of Fort Defiance. Fort Defiance had been built in 1851 in what is now Arizona as a defense against Navajo raids on local settlers, although the fort seemed superfluous after a peace agreement was reached in 1858. Reconciliation, however, was matched by an equal amount of mutual suspicion, and the US commander at Santa Fe, New Mexico, Colonel Benjamin Bonneville, made regular aggressive patrols around Fort Defiance, and also held 21 Indian prisoners as hostages against the treaty terms.

In January 1860, Navajo–American relations deteriorated, as the Indians began attacks on US supply trains and small isolated outposts. Then, on April 30, some 1,000 Navajo launched a massive attack on Fort Defiance. Reflecting the type of tactics described by Bourke (above), the assault came in from three directions, and managed to take some of the outlying buildings. Only the resistance of three companies of the 3rd Infantry prevented the Indians overrunning Fort Defiance completely, and after two hours of fighting the American troops managed to launch a counter-attack that eventually put the Indians to flight. The US troops had suffered three casualties during the battle, whereas the Navajo lost 12 killed and wounded. The casualties in the battle of Fort Defiance are remarkably light considering the numbers of warriors involved, but it illustrates how the Southwest Indians, as much as the Indians of any other territory, were reluctant to prosecute a battle of long duration, unlike many of the settler forces. It also illustrates how difficult the Indians found tackling well-arranged defenses, which here allowed the US troops to take full advantage of their superior firepower.

▲ **An Apache raiding party attacks a white settler family's home, burning the house and scalping members of the family. Such images, not always based on fact, inspired a vicious hostility toward the Indians.**

CHAPTER 4

WEAPONS

Conrad Malte-Brun painted a usefully broad picture of the weapons of the Apaches in the early 1800s, one which provides a context for analysis of Southwest Indians weaponry generally:

"The arrows of the Apaches are three feet [1m] long, and are made of reed or cane, into which they sink a piece of hard-wood, with a point made of iron, bone, or stone. The shot this weapon with such force, that at the distance of 300 paces they can pierce a man. When the arrow is attempted to be drawn out of the wound, the wood detaches itself, and the point remains in the body. Their second offensive weapon is a lance, fifteen feet [4.6m] long. When they charge the enemy they hold this lance with both hands above their head and, at the same time, guide their horse by pressing him with their knees.

▼ Navajo Indians gather at Fort Defiance, Arizona, circa 1873. The Navajo Indians actually managed to return to their homelands following the Navajo Treaty of 1868. Combined with good trade relations with the settlers, this return resulted in sustained population growth.

Many of them are armed with firelocks, which, as well as the ammunition, they have taken in battle from the Spaniards, who never sell them any. The archers and fusileers combat on foot; but the lancers are always on horseback. They make use of a buckler for defense.

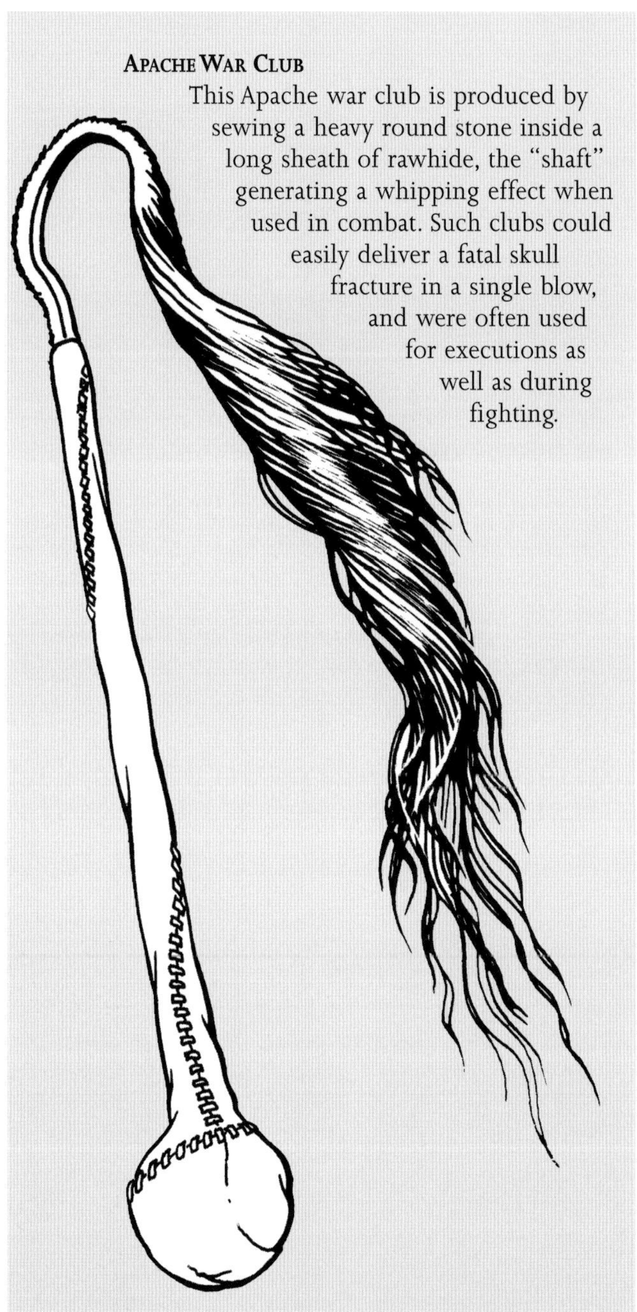

Apache War Club

This Apache war club is produced by sewing a heavy round stone inside a long sheath of rawhide, the "shaft" generating a whipping effect when used in combat. Such clubs could easily deliver a fatal skull fracture in a single blow, and were often used for executions as well as during fighting.

◀ San Juan, a Mescalero Apache chief, stands for his portrait holding a spear and a shield. The line across the shield indicates that it could fold down when not in use, and it is decorated with sun and star motifs. He wears a traditional chief's blanket.

Nothing can equal the impetuosity and address of their horsemen. They are thunderbolts, whose stroke it is impossible to parry or escape."

– *Malte-Brun* (1829)

Malte-Brun gives a largely accurate account of Apache weaponry and tactics, although with some errors, as we shall see. The traditional weapons of the Southwest Indians were the lance, club, sling, and bow, which they used to great effect even once they had widely adopted "firelocks" during the eighteenth century. Interestingly, the Southwest Indians also used rudimentary types of swords, at least until their value was lost during the battles against the far better-equipped Spaniards.

One type of sword was entirely wooden and shaped basically like a paddle, the broad edge of the paddle "sharpened" to form a rudimentary blade. The second principal type of sword had a little more sophistication, and consisted of a shaft around 3 feet (1 m) long with the edge studded with razor-sharp pieces of obsidian. In determined hands, such a sword was capable of severing a man's head with a single blow, but it still came a poor second to the steel blades of the Spanish *conquistadors*.

The lance is often overlooked in popular representations of the Native American at war, yet it was an integral part of their arsenal. A typical Apache lance would, as Malte-Brun notes, measure up to 15 ft. (4.6 m) long, and was capable of delivering a lethal penetrating wound to anybody caught on the end.

◀ This postcard of Geronimo is interesting for the close-up of the basic Apache war club. While some war clubs were sewn into hide (*see opposite*), a more rudimentary but equally effective form of club consisted of a rounded stone bound to the end of a shaft with rawhide thongs.

▲ **An Apache hunter procuring poison for his arrows by causing a rattlesnake to bite into a deer liver. Arrow heads were then dipped into the liver. Other poison sources included spiders and putrefied meat.**

Bows

Yet where Malte-Brun is in error is in his claim that archers would fight only on foot, and not from horseback. Although stalking and raiding tactics meant that this was true in many situations, eyewitness accounts have shown that the Apaches were indeed talented bowmen even from the back of a horse. George Catlin, an American painter, writer, and traveler who specialized in the Native Americans as his subject matter during the early 1800s, once witnessed a group of Apache warriors performing competitive archery from the back of galloping horses, and was impressed by both their speed and accuracy:

"For this day's sport, which is repeated many times in the year, the ground is chosen on the prairie, level and good for running, and in a semicircle are made ten successive circular targets in the ground by cutting away the turf, and making a sort of 'bull's-eye' in the center, covered with pipe-clay, which is white. Prizes are shot for, and judges are appointed to award them. Each warrior, mounted, in his war costume and war paint, and shoulders naked, and shield upon his back, takes ten arrows in his left hand with his bow, as if going into battle, and galloping their horse around in a circle of a mile or so, under full whip to get them at the highest speed, thus pass in succession the ten targets and give their arrows as they pass. The rapidity with which their arrows are placed upon the string and sent is a mystery to the bystander, and must be seen to be believed. No repeating arms every yet constructed are so rapid, nor any arm, and that little distance, more fatal."

– *Catlin (1868)*

▲ A young Navajo warrior with bow and arrows. The bow here is a simple piece of wood, probably yew, ash, or juniper, but some Southwest Indian tribes' bows were enhanced with strips of sinew to increase their elasticity and therefore improve the release velocity of the arrows.

The lethality and talent of the Apache archers is obvious, and it is inconceivable that they would not apply such skills in combat, as did tribes such as the Comanche. Malte-Brun's earlier account illustrates how the arrows themselves were designed for maximum physical impact, the sophisticated design including a detachable arrowhead to increase the severity of the wound.

In terms of bow design, the Indians of the southwest used both sinew-backed and self-bows, the latter made from woods such as juniper, yew, and ash. James Haley, in his book *Apaches: A History and Cultural Portrait* (1981), has shown how these bows had

Arrow Straightener
The arrow straightener was a piece of wood or horn bored through with perforations. Arrow shafts were passed through the apertures, and the implement used as a wrench to straighten out irregularities in the shaft.

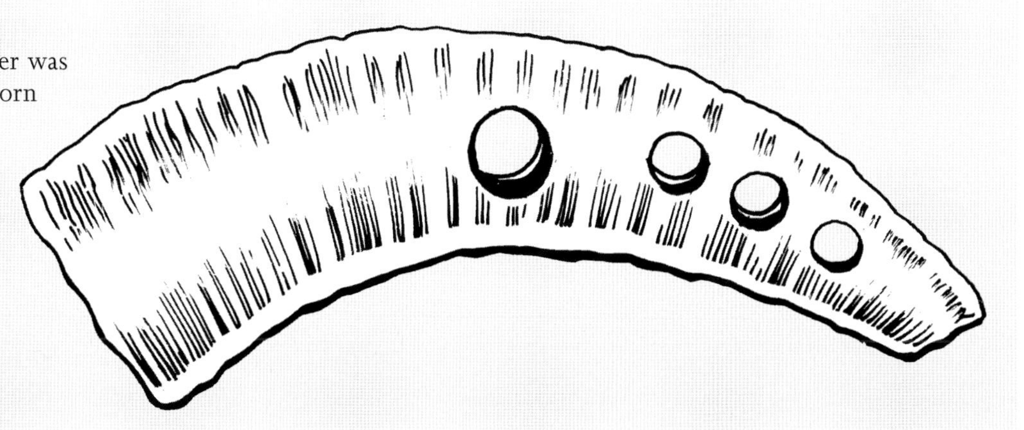

respectable power and range. He notes that a sinew-backed bow could fire an arrow at 141 ft. (43 m) per second and penetrate Spanish armor. But even the self-bow could accurately fire arrows at 115 ft. (35 m) per second to ranges of more than 328 ft. (100 m). Haley notes that "arrows striking a tree at short distance frequently drove into the wood until they were not removable—sometimes over halfway; deer shot at short range were usually run through and the arrows recovered beyond" (Haley, 1981).

Firearms

Of course, the Southwest Indians relented to the gradual infiltration of firearms. The Apache and other Southwest Indian tribes lived primarily as hunter-gathers, supplemented by some limited agriculture, and their diet was varied—it included deer, antelope, elk, rabbits, woodrats, and, in the eastern territories, buffalo. They also ate horses and mules when necessary. Firearms provided a new and highly successful tool for both hunting such diverse prey and for waging war. Furthermore, the prolific employment of Indians as scouts in the US forces meant that many Indians received formal training in the use of firearms, which helped wed them to the practicality of guns. Photographs of Indian warriors from the late nineteenth century reveal an inconsistent distribution of firearms throughout the Southwestern tribes. For example, a photograph of Geronimo and his associates just before his surrender to Crook in 1886 showed the Apaches carrying Springfield and Winchester rifles, various types of handguns as well as the traditional bows and arrows.

CHAPTER 5

SHIELDS AND ARMOR

Looking back at Malte-Brun's description of Apache warfare, we see his reference to Indian warriors using a "buckler"—a European term for a small shield. David Jones has observed that "the southwest fascination with shields equaled that of the Plains warriors and exceeded theirs in producing a greater variety of designs" (Jones, 2004). The constituent elements of the Southwestern shields were typically thick layers of rawhide (horse or bison) or buckskin often stretched over the disk of wood, although in some instances the wood was omitted and the layers of skin simply multiplied to compensate.

A typical Navajo shield, for example, consisted of two thick layers of hide, shaped to measure about 18 inches (46 centimeters) in diameter when dried. Heavy rawhide stitching was sometimes applied around the rim to strengthen the construction. In some instances, the shield was creased down the middle and capable of being folded away when not in use. The shield was gripped by a small wooden handle. Jones notes that, in the case of the Apaches, "when fighting on foot with a shield, they were trained to crouch low and extend the shield before them so that they almost disappeared from view as they approached the enemy" (Jones, 2004).

On occasion, particularly during the early inter-tribal battles when no firearms were present, sometimes just a hefty buckskin sufficed to provide a basic shield. In 1928,

◀ Apaches with percussion cap carbines, late nineteenth century. During this century, Native Americans were keen to get their hands on rifled weapons, which they appreciated for their greater accuracy in hunting and combat.

▶ **Fort Wingate, New Mexico. Apache scouts drill with rifles. US Army firearms issued to Native Americans were of variable quality. Many guns were old flintlock muskets crudely rifled and converted to the percussion cap system.**

Leslie Spier wrote an article for the *Anthropological Papers of the American Museum of Natural History*, entitled "Havasupai Ethnography." In it he described a raid by Yavapai Indians on a Havasupai camp. During the battle, the Havasupai showed an ingenious use of buckskins as an *ad hoc* form of protection. For stopping arrows, they would drape a large piece of buckskin over a stick or bow, holding it up in front of them as a form of shield. The loose-hanging sheet of hide, even if it didn't entirely stop the passage of an arrow, would certainly alter its course and subtract from its power, providing what modern military engineers would call "stand-off distance" between the shield and the individual behind it. Furthermore, at one point, the group of Yavapai were trapped and resorted to hurling stones at the Havasupai, which once again were parried by the buckskin shields. Jones notes that "a number of times, the others were sent back to the Havasupai camp for more deerskins, as the ones in use lost their effectiveness after absorbing rocks and arrows for a number of hours" (Jones, 2004).

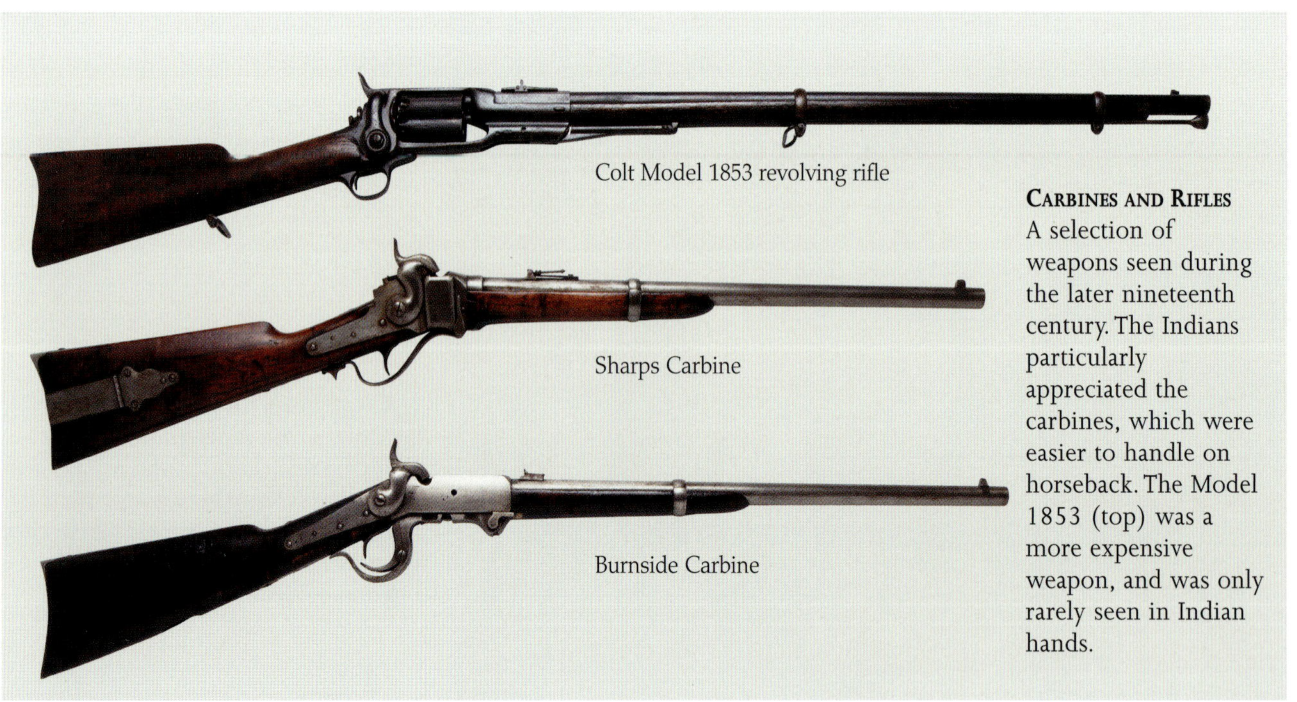

Carbines and Rifles
A selection of weapons seen during the later nineteenth century. The Indians particularly appreciated the carbines, which were easier to handle on horseback. The Model 1853 (top) was a more expensive weapon, and was only rarely seen in Indian hands.

Apache Warrior with Shield
An Apache warrior crouches down to recce the land before him. He clutches a small round medicine shield; these shields were typically capable of stopping arrows and spears.

In addition to carrying shields, the Southwest Indians also used body armor to protect themselves in battle. Typically this armor was formed by wrapping layers of hide around the torso, such as was typical of the Hopi Indians, or by creating buckskin warshirts, as seen among the various Apache tribes. These warshirts could be particularly hefty, built up from as many as eight layers of thick buckskin, the layers glued together by a powerful adhesive made from cactus leaves. The shirts often had elbow-length sleeves, providing some measure of protection for the arms while in close-quarters combat, but without hampering mobility.

Generally speaking, the heaviest specimens of shirt were worn by mounted warriors (these warshirts often extended to knee length and incorporated splits to allow the warrior to mount and dismount his horse), while the lighter varieties were naturally favored by those who had to travel and fight on foot.

Medicine Shield
The medicine shield above is replete with Apache symbolism. The prevalence of circles is tied to the Apache "sacred hoop," a symbol of the circle of life from birth to death. Also represented here are teepees and phases of the moon.

The Hopi Indians

The Hopi Indians feature little in this chapter, as their physical isolation in tough territories of Arizona, plus their frequent willingness to engage with settler culture, meant that they were largely preserved from the murderous battles of the nineteenth century. During the sixteenth century, however, they came into conflict with the expanding Spanish, particularly against the depredations of the explorer Francisco de Coronado, who in 1541 led a campaign of conquest into Hopi territory. The Hopi put up a patchy resistance to Spanish encroachment, but attempts to convert them to Christianity intensified the fightback, and the Hopi joined in the Pueblo Rebellion of 1680. When this eventually failed, the Hopi relocated many of their settlements to more inaccessible parts of the country, where they continued their attempt to practice their traditional way of life in the face of settler expansion.

Hopi rabbit stick

▲ A group of Hopi Indians are seen here on a hunting trip, simply armed with spears and rabbit sticks. The rabbit stick was a curved piece of heavy wood, designed to bring down not only rabbits but also other small game and even coyotes. It was thrown at the target animal in a low skimming action, parallel to the ground, and would deliver a stunning blow if it struck.

Geronimo's "Mightiest Battle"

The autobiography of Geronimo has proved invaluable for illuminating our understanding of Southwest Indian warrior culture. A fitting way to end this chapter is to examine what Geronimo termed his "Mightiest Battle," which occurred during the mid-1880s in Mexico, when Geronimo was once more on the run with his band of followers. His account of this battle pulls together some of threads of this chapter, and provides a good overall picture of how the Southwest Indians coped with a variety of tactical challenges.

The story opens with Geronimo and his followers "camped in the mountains north of Arispe" (all the quotations given here are from the previously cited Barrett autobiography):

"One night we made camp some distance from the mountains by a stream. There was not much water in the stream, but a deep channel was worn through the prairie, and small trees were beginning to grow here and there along the bank of this stream."

"In those days we never camped without placing scouts, for we knew that we were liable to be attacked at any time. The next morning just at daybreak our scouts came in, aroused the camp, and notified us that Mexican troops were approaching. Within five minutes the Mexicans began firing on us. We took to the ditches made by the stream, and had the women and children busy digging these deeper. I gave strict orders to waste no ammunition and keep under cover. We killed many Mexicans that day and in turn lost heavily, for the fight lasted all day. Frequently troops would charge at one point, be repulsed then rally and charge at another point."

Geronimo's use of security and firepower reads as if written in a military instruction manual. It is apparent that scouts not only acted in tracking and reconnaissance roles during missions, but also as sentries around the perimeter of a camp. Responding to the Mexican fire, Geronimo also gets his people to occupy proper positions of cover, and the auxiliary role of the women and children is particularly interesting, showing how an entire community could contribute to the battle. He also respects the issue of ammunition conservation, already noted earlier in this chapter, and it is likely that simply remaining under cover resulted in diminishing Mexican fire, as they became conscious of their own ammunition depletion. About midday, the Mexicans obviously began to review their options:

"About noon we began to hear them speaking my name with curses. In the afternoon the general came on the field and the fighting became more furious. I gave orders to my warriors to try to kill all the Mexican officers. About three o'clock the general called all the

▲ **A captive white boy in an Apache camp.**

▲ **Geronimo and his braves in battle order.**

officers together at the right side of the field. The place where they assembled was not very far from the main stream and a little ditch ran out close to where the officers stood. Cautiously I crawled out of this ditch very close to where the council was being held. The general was an old warrior. The wind was blowing in my direction, so that I could hear all he said, and I understood most of it. This is about what he told them: 'Officers, yonder in those ditches is the red devil Geronimo and his hated band. This must be his last day. Ride on him from both sides of the ditches; kill men, women, and children; take no prisoners; dead Indians are what we want. Do not spare your own men; exterminate this band at any cost; I will post the wounded and shoot all deserters; go back to your companies and advance.'"

"Kill the Mexican Officers"

Allowing for some license on the part of the translator, or Geronimo's memory, the Mexicans apparently realized that exchanging fire at a distance from positions of cover was no way to settle the battle with Geronimo. From the Indian point of view, note how Geronimo gives instructions to his warriors to "kill all the Mexican officers." His understanding of Mexican command-and-control, highly centralized upon the officers, is apparent, no doubt aided by his ability to understand the Spanish language. At this point, Geronimo took matters into his own hands as he decapitated the Spanish force and began the battle:

"Just as the command to go forward was given I took deliberate aim at the general and he fell. In an instant the ground around me was riddled with bullets; but I was untouched. The Apaches had seen. From all along the ditches arose the fierce war-cry of my people. The columns wavered an instant and then swept on; they did not retreat until our fire had destroyed the front ranks."

"After this their fighting was not so fierce, yet they continued to rally and readvance until dark. They also continued to speak my name with threats and curses. That night before the firing had ceased a dozen Indians had crawled out of the ditches and set fire to the long prairie grass behind the Mexican troops. During the confusion that followed we escaped to the mountains."

Geronimo's killing of the Mexican general seems to establish a tactical and morale advantage in the coming battle, but it still takes disciplined Indian firepower to cut down the Mexican attack. Yet ultimately, Geronimo does not take the fighting to the ultimate conclusion of destroying the enemy force. Instead, sensing that enough work has been done, he creates a fire as a diversion and makes his escape.

This battle is an extraordinary picture of Indian coordination, intelligence, and martial spirit. As with so many other Indian battles, the critical command decisions revolve as much around knowing when to withdraw and when to fight, which explains how the Southwest Indians were able to hold out against overwhelming forces for so long.

▲ **Geronimo and Natchez.**

▲ **Geronimo, his son, and two picked braves.**

Glossary

acute Perceptive.
atrocity A very cruel or horrible act.
belligerent Aggressive or hostile.
buckskin The preserved hide of an animal, usually deer, which is soft, flexible, and can be used for a variety of things, including clothing, bags, and shields.
casualties Lives lost to war or other devastating circumstances.
defile Narrow passageways through or between hills, mountains, or rocks.
depletion Reduction in the supply of something.
depredation The act of plundering or attacking.
encroachment Invasion of another's territory.
etiquette A code of behavior customary to particular rituals or groups.
incessant Persisting without interruption.
lethality The capacity for something to be fatal or cause death.
marksman A person skilled at shooting a target with a ranged weapon.
martial Having to do with war; warlike.
pitiablc Evoking pity.
prestigious Well-respected or admired.
prolific Plentiful or abundant.
proposition A suggested course of action.
raid A surprise assault on a group.
recce To scout out an area and become more familiar with it.
rendezvous An agreed-upon time and place to meet.
rudimentary Basic.
shaman Someone who is considered to be in tune with the spiritual world and can offer guidance and protection through various rituals.
skirmish A short, spontaneous fight during a war.
stupefaction A state of surprise or shock.

Further Reading

Alvarez, Alex. *Native America and the Question of Genocide.* Lanham, MD: Rowman & Littlefield, 2016.

Hutton, Paul Andrew. *The Apache Wars: The Hunt for Geronimo, the Apache Kid, and the Captive Boy Who Started the Longest War in American History.* New York, NY: Crown, 2016.

King, J. C. H. *Blood and Land: The Story of Native North America*. London, UK: Penguin UK, 2016.

Kuiper, Kathleen. *American Indians of California, the Great Basin, and the Southwest* (Native American Tribes). New York, NY: Britannica Educational Publishing, 2012.

Leahy, Todd, and Nathan Wilson. *Historical Dictionary of Native American Movements.* Lanham, MD: Rowman & Littlefield, 2016.

Neitzel, Jill E. *Recognizing People in the Prehistoric Southwest.* Salt Lake City, UT: University of Utah Press, 2017.

Richmond, Wren. *Apache* (Spotlight On Native Americans). New York, NY: PowerKids Press, 2016.

Roberts, David. *The Lost World of the Old Ones: Discoveries in the Ancient Southwest.* New York, NY: W. W. Norton & Company, 2015.

Sanford, William R. *Apache Chief Geronimo* (Native American Chiefs and Warriors). New York, NY: Enslow Publishing, 2013.

Zappia, Natale A. *Traders and Raiders: The Indigenous World of the Colorado Basin, 1540–1859.* Chapel Hill, NC: The University of North Carolina Press, 2014.

Websites

National Museum of the American Indian Collections Search
http://www.nmai.si.edu/searchcollections/home.aspx

The Smithsonian National Museum of the American Indian's online collection contains images of a vast array of Indian artifacts and art, both contemporary and historical. The collection is searchable by culture, region, artist, and object specifications and contains detailed information on the objects' history and material qualities.

Native Languages of the Americas: Native American Indian Weapons
http://www.native-languages.org/weapons.htm
This gallery displays a wide variety of Native American weapons from different tribes across the Americas, as well as links to further resources regarding relevant weapons, armor, and war traditions.

WWW Virtual Library – American Indians
http://www.hanksville.org/NAresources
This up-to-date database contains an expansive index of Native American online resources, including links to information on oral and written histories, different forms of media, and special government organizations for indigenous peoples.

INDEX